BEN NIGHTHORSE CAMPBELL

Senator and Artist

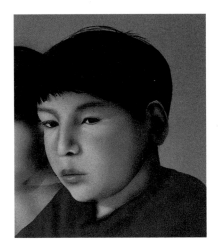

Written by Nuchi Nashoba
Illustrated by Timoteo Ikoshy Montoya

MODERN CURRICULUM PRESS

Program Reviewers

Cathy White Eagle, Executive Director
and President of the Board
Eagle Vision Educational Network
Granite Bay, California

Jeffrey Hamley, Director
Native American Program
Harvard University
Cambridge, Massachusetts

Gwen Sebastian Hill, Teacher
Development Trainer
District of Philadelphia
Philadelphia, Pennsylvania

Paulette Molin, Ph.D., Assistant Dean
The Graduate College
Hampton University
Hampton, Virginia

Joan Webkamigad, Education Specialist
Michigan Department of Education
Lansing, Michigan

Executive Editor: Janet Rosenthal
Project Editors: Elizabeth Wojnar
Mark Shelley

MODERN CURRICULUM PRESS

An imprint of Paramount Supplemental Education
250 James Street
Morristown, New Jersey 07960

ISBN 0-8136-5757-1   (Reinforced Binding)   0-8136-5763-6   (Paperback)
Library of Congress Catalog Card Number: 94-077296

10 9 8 7 6 5 4 3 2 1   SP   99 98 97 96 95 94

Dear Reader,

Ben Nighthorse Campbell had a difficult childhood. But he didn't let that stop him from reaching his goals.

Today, as a member of the United States Congress, Senator Campbell helps fight for Native American rights.

Read to find out how Ben overcame rough times to grow up to set an example for all Americans, especially Native American people. Like Ben, we should all be proud of our heritage.

Your friend,

Ouchi Olashoba

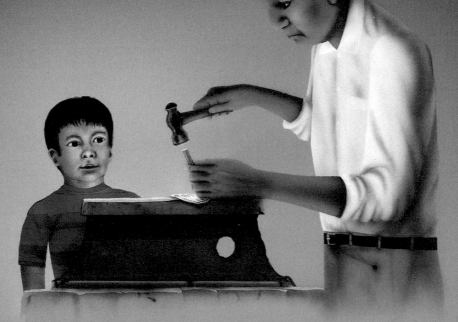

Three-year-old Ben Campbell stood
behind his father in their California
home. He couldn't take his eyes off of
his father's hands. Albert Campbell's
fingers quickly shaped a piece of silver.
Albert, who was a member of the
Northern Cheyenne Nation, made
beautiful pieces of jewelry. To Ben it
seemed like magic.

Ben spent many happy hours watching his father make jewelry. But other times were not as happy. Ben's father had a disease called alcoholism. This made it hard for him to care for Ben and Alberta, Ben's older sister.

Ben's mother, Mary, tried her best to care for her children. But she had a disease, too. Her disease was called tuberculosis.

In 1938, when Ben was five years old, his mother had to go to the hospital. Ben and Alberta went to live in an orphanage, or a home for children. The Campbells were very sad that their family could not be together. This was a hard time for all of them.

Ben and Alberta stayed in the orphanage for six months. They returned home when their parents were able to take care of them. This was not the end of their sad times, however. Over the next ten years, Ben and Alberta stayed in orphanages many times.

Ben does have some happy memories of his childhood. When he was twelve, his father taught him how to make Native American jewelry. Ben loved making beautiful things out of coins and pieces of silver.

8

When Ben was a teenager, he began getting into trouble. He missed many days of school. Often he would fight with other people.

Ben was not happy with the way he was acting. He began working at many different jobs after school. At one job, Ben took care of cattle. He also worked at an orchard, or fruit farm, picking fruit.

While at the orchard, Ben became friends with some of the Japanese people who worked there. Ben watched as they practiced the sport of Judo. He asked his new friends to teach him judo. He was excited when they agreed.

PACIFIC

OCEAN

KOREA

JAPAN

U.S.A.

CALIFORNIA

In 1950, when Ben was seventeen
years old, he left high school. A few
months later, Ben joined the Air Force
and went to Korea.

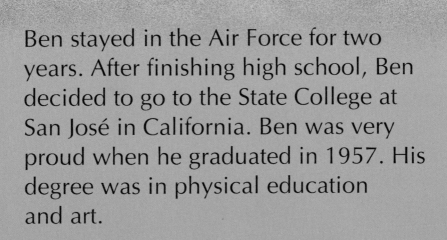

Ben stayed in the Air Force for two
years. After finishing high school, Ben
decided to go to the State College at
San José in California. Ben was very
proud when he graduated in 1957. His
degree was in physical education
and art.

In 1960, Ben moved to Tokyo, Japan to study judo. Three years later he won a gold medal at the Pan-American Games. In 1964, he was chosen as the captain of the first United States judo team for the Olympics. Ben finished in fourth place even with a knee injury!

15

A few years later, Ben moved back to California to teach judo. In 1966, he married Linda Price. Ben had met Linda while he was teaching. They later had a son, Colin, and a daughter, Shanan.

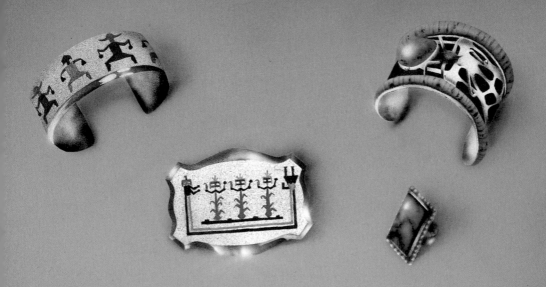

For the next ten years, Ben worked at many different jobs. He continued to teach judo and even wrote a book about it. Ben also taught Native Americans how to make jewelry. Teaching the class made Ben think about his own Native American heritage, or history.

Ben became very interested in the Cheyenne Nation. He learned about his great-grandfather, whose name was Blackhorse. The Cheyenne Nation honored Ben by giving him the name Nighthorse. In the Cheyenne language, Nighthorse means the same as Blackhorse.

19

In 1977, Ben moved his family to
Ignacio, Colorado. Ben bought a
ranch and raised horses and cattle. He
also managed a rodeo arena and
continued to make beautiful jewelry.

Ben's concern for the people of Colorado led him to run for public office. In 1982, he was elected to the Colorado legislature. In 1986, he was elected to Congress. Ben was the only Native American to serve in Congress that term. Then, in 1992, Ben was elected a senator from Colorado.

23

As a senator, Ben Nighthorse Campbell wants to let everyone know about Native Americans and the problems they face. With his help, a bill was passed in Congress creating the National Museum of the American Indian in Washington, D.C.

Ben has learned a lot from the hard times that he has faced throughout his life. He has advice for young people: "Be proud. But above all, do something to be remembered." Ben Nighthorse Campbell has taken his own advice. He will surely be remembered.

Glossary

elect (ē lekt′) to choose a leader of a group by having the members of the group vote for one person. The business of voting is called an **election**. The person who gets the most votes is **elected**.

government (guv′ərn mənt) all the people and agencies that run or control a city, state, or country

rodeo arena (rō′dē o ə rē′nə) a large place where horse shows and other events can take place

Senator (sen′ ə tər) a person who is elected to the Senate

tuberculosis (to͞o bʉr′kyo͞o lō′sis) a sickness of the lungs

United States Congress (kän′grəs) the branch of government that makes the laws. Congress is made up of the House of Representatives and the Senate.

About the Author

Nuchi Nashoba is a member of the Choctaw Nation from Southeastern Oklahoma. In 1984, she represented Native Americans as a Goodwill Ambassador to the summer Olympic Games in Los Angeles. Ms. Nashoba is dedicated to keeping the tradition and culture of the Choctaw alive. To teach her three children, Ben, Tanchi, and Tana, about their Native American heritage, Ms. Nashoba writes short stories for them.

About the Illustrator

Timoteo Ikoshy Montoya is a self-taught artist of Mescalaro Apache and Chicano descent. He believes that Senator Campbell's struggles are something that Native Americans and artists can relate to. Ikoshy lives in California with his wife, Nadine, and two children, Teo and Raina. In *Ben Nighthorse Campbell,* Ikoshy used airbrush to celebrate the senator's achievements.

MAR 1 0 1998